If any, upon being denounced and convicted of the sin of heresy, shall deny and persist in his denial until sentence is passed, . . . the inquisitors must declare him a heretic and so sentence him. . . . If the said crime of heresy or apostasy is half-proven the inquisitors may . . . [put] the accused to the torture.

Tomás de Torquemada,
**Official Instructions of
the Spanish Inquisition,
Articles XIV and XV**

This book is for Allan and Leonore.

Photographs © 2008: age fotostock: 36 (Markus Bassler/Bidarchiv Monheim), 117 (Juan José Pascual); akg-Images, London: 54 (The British Library), 65 top, 112; Alamy Images: 10 (PopperFoto), 20 (Mick Rock/Cephas Picture Library), 66 bottom, 79 (The Print Collector); Art Resource, NY: 108 (Bildarchiv Preussischer Kulturbesitz), 26 (Werner Forman), 64 top (Réunion des Musées Nationaux), 73 (Snark); Bridgeman Art Library International Ltd., London/New York: 64 center (Bibliothèque Nationale, Paris, France), 65 bottom (Bibliothèque Nationale, Paris, France/ Giraudon), 29 (Museo Diocesano de Barcelona, Spain/Index), 62 top (Paul Maeyaert/Valladolid, Spain); Corbis Images: 63 top, 89 (Archivo Iconografico, S.A.), 59, 83 (Bettmann), 46, 63 bottom (Stefano Bianchetti); Courtesy Jewish Public Library, Montreal, Canada: 66 top, 67 top; Mary Evans Picture Library: 52; The Art Archive/Picture Desk/Dagli Orti/Museo del Prado: 38, 39, 67 bottom; The British Library/Or. 2884: 22; The Image Works: 64 bottom (AAAC/Topham), 87, 92 (Mary Evans Picture Library), 62 bottom (The British Library/HIP), 33 (Topham).

Illustrations by XNR Productions, Inc.: 4, 5, 8, 9
Cover art by Mark Summers
Chapter art for chapters 2, 4, 7, 9, 10, 12 by Roland Sarkany
Chapter art for introduction and chapters 1, 3, 5, 6, 8, 11, 13, 14, 15 by Raphael Montoliu

Library of Congress Cataloging-in-Publication Data

Goldberg, Enid A.
Tomás de Torquemada : architect of torture during the Spanish Inquisition /
Enid A. Goldberg and Norman Itzkowitz.
p. cm. — (A wicked history)
Includes bibliographical references and index.
ISBN-13: 978-0-531-12598-4 (lib. bdg.) 978-0-531-13897-7 (pbk.)
ISBN-10: 0-531-12598-X (lib. bdg.) 0-531-13897-7 (pbk.)
1. Torquemada, Tomás de, 1420-1498. 2. Dominicans—Spain—Biography. 3.
Inquisition—Spain. I. Itzkowitz, Norman. II. Title.
BX4705.T7G65 2007
272'.2092—dc22
[B]

2007012931

Tod Olson, Series Editor
Marie O'Neill, Art Director
SimonSays Design!, Design and Production

© 2008 Scholastic Inc.

All rights reserved. Published by Franklin Watts, an imprint of Scholastic Inc.
Published simultaneously in Canada. Printed in the United States of America. 23

SCHOLASTIC, FRANKLIN WATTS, and associated logos are
trademarks and/or registered trademarks of Scholastic Inc.

1 2 3 4 5 6 7 8 9 10 R 17 16 15 14 13 12 11 10 09 08

A WiCKED HISTORY™

Tomás de Torquemada

Architect of Torture During the Spanish Inquisition

ENID A. GOLDBERG &
NORMAN ITZKOWITZ

Franklin Watts
An Imprint of Scholastic Inc.
New York   Toronto   London   Auckland   Sydney
Mexico City   New Delhi   Hong Kong
Danbury, Connecticut

Torquemada's World

With help from King Ferdinand and Queen Isabella, Tomás de Torquema
spread the Inquisition through the land known today as Spain.

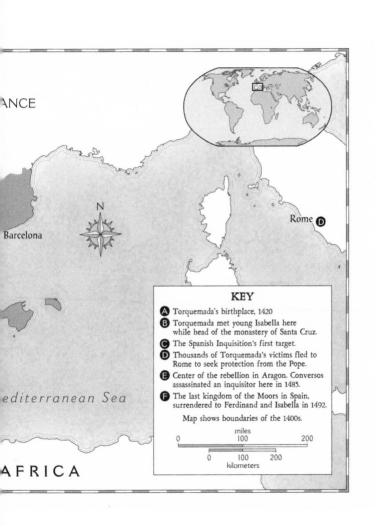

ANCE

Barcelona

N

Rome **D**

editerranean Sea

AFRICA

KEY

A Torquemada's birthplace, 1420

B Torquemada met young Isabella here
while head of the monastery of Santa Cruz.

C The Spanish Inquisition's first target.

D Thousands of Torquemada's victims fled to
Rome to seek protection from the Pope.

E Center of the rebellion in Aragon. Conversos
assassinated an inquisitor here in 1485.

F The last kingdom of the Moors in Spain,
surrendered to Ferdinand and Isabella in 1492.

Map shows boundaries of the 1400s.

miles
0   100   200

0   100   200
kilometers

TABLE OF CONTENTS

A Wicked Web

A look at the allies and enemies of Tomás de Torquemada.

World Leaders

KING FERDINAND —— QUEEN ISABELLA
Ruler of Aragon   Ruler of Castile

POPE SIXTUS IV
head of the Catholic Church

Influential Jewish Leaders

ISAAC ABRAVANEL
a financier

ABRAHAM SENIOR
treasurer to the crown

TOMÁS DE TORQUEMADA

Inquisitors

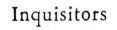

PEDRO ARBUÉS DE EPILA
in Aragon (killed in Saragossa)

GASPAR JUGLAR
in Aragon

Anti-Jewish Preachers

FERRANT MARTÍNEZ
spread fear throughout the south
of Spain

VINCENT FERRER
converted thousands of Jews to
Christianity

ALONSO DE SPINA
wrote a book attacking Jews
and conversos

ALONSO DE HOJEDA
a Dominican from Seville

TOMÁS DE TORQUEMADA (1420–1498)

DON ISAAC ABRAVANEL SAT IN THE ALHAMBRA PALACE OF GRANADA. Across a heavy wooden table sat the rulers of Spain. King Ferdinand and Queen Isabella had good reason to be pleased with Abravanel. They had just won a long and costly war. The region of Granada was now in their hands. Abravanel, a Jewish financier, had given a large part of his fortune to make it happen.

Many Spanish Jews helped pay for the war. And the results were splendid. Ferdinand and Isabella could see for themselves. All they had to do was look around at the Alhambra. The walls of their room rose 75 feet to a white, blue, and gold dome. Rays of light shone in from nine large windows. Brightly colored tiles covered the walls. The Alhambra was a work of art. Thanks in part to Abravanel, it now belonged to Spain.

But Abravanel hadn't come to the Alhambra to receive thanks. He knew that Ferdinand and Isabella had other things on their minds. The king and queen felt that Spanish Jews had become a danger to their Christian nation. They wanted to push all Jews out of Spain.

Don Isaac had come to Granada to save his people.

Abravanel and another Jewish leader, Don Abraham Senior, pleaded with Ferdinand and Isabella. They listed the services Jews had provided to the crown. Many held high positions in government. Don Abraham himself was the court treasurer. They also promised that Jews would obey the strict Spanish laws. They would stay in the Jewish neighborhoods, or ghettos, at night. They would avoid mixing with Christians.

Finally, Don Isaac and Don Abraham made their last offer. They laid a bag of gold on the table. According to one account, they let the coins roll and jingle to tempt the king. The money amounted to 30,000 Spanish ducats—over 3,000 ounces of gold. If Ferdinand let the Jews stay, the gold would be his.

The king considered the offer. If the Jews left Spain, he could seize their possessions. But if they stayed, he could force them to keep paying taxes, year after year. Ferdinand began to waver.

Just then, the door burst open. An old man stormed into the room. He wore a black cloak over white robes. His head was shaved in the style of a monk, with a ring of hair around the temples. His face was twisted with rage.

If the story is true, Don Isaac and Don Abraham must have lost hope at the sight. The angry friar was Tomás de Torquemada, the most feared man in Spain. For ten years, Torquemada had led a brutal fight against those who were considered enemies of the Catholic Church. As leader of the Spanish Inquisition, he sent spies to the far corners of Spain. His spies turned friends against friends. They made sons and daughters testify against their parents. They tortured suspects until a person would confess to anything.

Now, Torquemada turned his rage on the Jews. He reminded the king and queen that Jesus had been betrayed for money. A follower named Judas took a bribe from Jesus' Roman enemies. Judas then led the Romans to Jesus, who was nailed to a cross to die.

"Judas sold Jesus for 30 pieces of silver," the monk shouted at the Spanish rulers. "You are about to sell him again for 30,000 ducats." He tore a wooden crucifix from around his neck. He threw it on the table with the gold. "Here He is. Take Him and sell Him. But don't blame me. I want no part of this business."

Torquemada left the room. The king and queen said nothing. Don Isaac and Don Abraham gathered their gold and left the palace. Their friends and families had to prepare for the worst.

If the legend is true, Torquemada had just put on a chilling performance. He forced thousands of people from their homes with a single speech. What kind of man could inspire such a story? Why did he hate—and fear—the Jews of Spain? And how did he use that hatred to launch one of the most brutal periods in the world's history?

PART 1

A Hound

of the

Lord

CHAPTER 1

Pure Blood?

As a boy, Tomás begins his search for A PURE RELIGIOUS LIFE.

TOMÁS DE TORQUEMADA, ARCHENEMY of the Jews, had a secret. He may have kept it his entire life. At the very least, he avoided talking about it. People around him may have whispered it to each other. But it's doubtful that anyone dared to speak the secret out loud. Still, according to Queen Isabella's historian, it was true: Torquemada himself was descended from Jews.

In other times, it would have been nothing to hide. But these were not ordinary times. And Torquemada was largely responsible.

Torquemada was the fanatical leader of the Spanish Inquisition. The Inquisition served as police, judge, and jury for the Catholic Church in Spain. And the Catholic Church was everywhere. It was the only legal Christian church in the country. Its rules were the law of the land. All Christians had to obey them. Christians who broke church rules weren't just considered sinners. They were criminals.

The Inquisition's judges set up courts in cities across the land. They hunted for heretics—any Christians who rejected the teachings of the church. And Christians with Jewish ancestors were the first suspects. They were said to have "impure blood." Every detail of their lives were examined. Had they ever doubted that God exists? Did they keep Jewish friends? Did they still practice Jewish customs? Suspects who were found guilty could be burned alive.

Fear became a way of life in Spain. Secrets were the key to survival.

The man who spread this fear across Spain was born in 1420. Tomás de Torquemada's family was an important one around the city of Valladolid. His relatives owned land. Some of them held jobs at the king's court. Tomás's uncle, Juan de Torquemada, was a cardinal, a leader in the Catholic Church.

Tomás' had one sister. As an only son, he was the family's only chance to pass their name on to future generations. But instead of marrying, Tomás decided to

TOMÁS GREW UP near Valladolid. The city was protected by the imposing Castle of Penafiel.

devote his life to God and become a friar. At an early age, he entered the Catholic school of San Pablo in Valladolid. He studied the Bible and the great Christian writers. And he lived under strict religious rules. He would never marry. He ate no meat. He walked barefoot. He refused as many comforts as he could.

Tomás wanted a strict, Catholic life. But the world around Tomás was not as strict, or as Catholic, as he would have liked. Muslims from North Africa— Moors, as the Europeans called them—had conquered much of Spain in the 700s. Little by little, Christian armies had been taking it back.

In many places, Jews, Muslims, and Christians lived side by side. And for many years, the three groups got along. In some towns, they shared public bathhouses. In Toledo, in the 1200s, they shared a church. Muslims worshipped on Friday, Jews on Saturday, and Christians on Sunday. Many Christians went to Jewish doctors. They bought clothes from Jewish tailors. They paid taxes to

Jewish tax collectors. In Valladolid, Jews, Christians, and Muslims all sold their goods in the main square on market days.

Most Jews lived apart from Christians in their own section of town. Tomás surely knew where the gates to the Valladolid ghetto were. Behind the gates, Jews lived according to their own customs. They worshipped on Saturday, not Sunday. They sang religious songs and

A JEWISH FAMILY in Spain celebrates the holiday of Passover. This scene was painted in the mid-1300s, when Jews could still worship in relative peace.

chanted in Hebrew. They prepared food by kosher rules. Pork was forbidden. They did not eat milk products and meat together. They even lived under their own legal code.

For many years Jewish families lived in peace. But they never forgot who was in charge. Jews made up only about two percent of the population. Spanish Christians controlled the courts and the armies. In the 1300s, some cities passed laws against the Jews. Jews were not allowed to marry Christians. They were barred from certain jobs. They had to wear colored patches on their shirts to identify themselves.

Most of the time, the laws were not enforced. But Jews got the message: If they lived in peace, it was because their powerful neighbors wanted it that way. At any moment, the Spanish Christians could shatter the peace.

That's exactly what happened one hot summer, 30 years before Tomás was born.

A DIVIDED SPAIN

WHILE TORQUEMADA WAS GROWING UP, Spain was not yet one country. It was split into two main kingdoms. Castile occupied the central part of the country. Aragon lay to the east. A smaller kingdom, called Navarre, hung onto its independence in the northeast. All three kingdoms were led by Christian rulers.

For centuries, Muslim leaders had dominated the area. Slowly, Christian armies in Castile and Aragon had reclaimed land from the Muslims. By the mid-1400s, only a small region in the south, called Granada, remained in Muslim hands.

Spanish Christians once again dominated the area. Jews and Muslims still lived all across the land. But many people dreamed of a united Spain devoted only to the Catholic Church.

THE MAP on pages 4–5 shows what Torquemada's Spain looked like.

24

Riot!

Violence forces thousands of Jews to GIVE UP THEIR FAITH.

IN THE SPRING OF 1391, three decades before Tomás's birth, signs of danger reached the Jewish ghettos. A fanatical preacher named Ferrant Martínez traveled through the south of Spain. He shouted lies from church pulpits across the land. He told crowds of Christians that the Jews were dangerous. The Jews had killed Jesus, he insisted. They poisoned wells and started plagues. They murdered Christians whenever they got the chance. A friar named Vincent Ferrer spread similar lies in Aragon to the east.

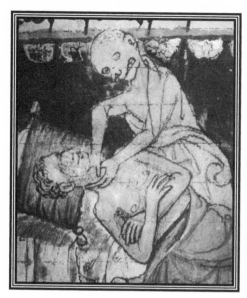

DEATH STRANGLES another plague victim. The Black Death killed 20 million Europeans in the mid-1400s. It inspired some gruesome art and also led to the persecution of thousands of Jews.

Word of these fiery sermons drifted into the ghettos. Jews prepared for the worst. And in June, the violence began. Riots struck the city of Seville first. Angry Christians charged into the Jewish ghetto. They murdered hundreds of people in their homes. The mob left the ghetto in ruins.

The terror spread quickly. Mobs stormed Jewish ghettos in Córdoba, Toledo, and other towns. In July, rioters killed 250 Jews in Valencia. In August,

Christians murdered 400 more in Barcelona. The violence finally ended in the fall.

While the memories were still fresh, Vincent Ferrer went to work. He arrived at Jewish synagogues waving a cross. He asked the Jews to become Christians. God would punish those who did not, he said.

Many Jews refused to convert. But some who had lived through the riots had seen enough punishment. They didn't care whether the violence came from God or people. They were tired of being called "Jewish dogs" and getting stoned in the streets. They were sick of fearing for their lives. They wanted to live in peace. So they began to convert to Christianity.

In the following years, thousands of Jews gave up their religion. The grandfather of Isaac Abravanel—the man who confronted Ferdinand and Isabella—was one of them. His name was Samuel, and he had been a financial advisor to three kings. But even he didn't feel safe from the violence. He decided to convert to Christianity.

The new converts were known as *conversos*, or New Christians. Conversos mixed with "old" Christians. In some places they earned high positions in society. They were free to marry Christians. Tomás's grandfather probably met and married a converso woman around this time.

But many Old Christians refused to accept the conversos. Some people called them *marranos*, which meant something like "pigs." Old Christians insisted that Jewish blood was "unclean." Christians had bright red blood, it was said. Jewish blood was supposed to be muddy in color.

Conversos tried hard to prove that they were true Christians. They went to church on Sunday. They learned verses from the Christian Bible. But some people speculated about what they did in private. Some conversos, it was said, still worshipped as Jews. They lit candles before sundown on Friday night. They refused to work on Saturday. They prayed secretly on the Jewish holy days.

By the 1450s, conversos were a big part of Spanish life. Tomás de Torquemada was in his thirties then. Like his uncle, he was a rising star in the Catholic Church. Juan de Torquemada, however, had defended the conversos in his writings. His nephew would soon become their biggest enemy.

JEWISH AND MUSLIM CONVERTS observe their new religion. This scene from a church altarpiece shows conversos as willing and faithful worshippers.

CHAPTER 3

Holier than Thou

TOMÁS MAKES A NAME FOR HIMSELF as a Dominican friar.

As A YOUNG MAN, TORQUEMADA finished his religious studies at San Pablo's. He then entered a monastery in the nearby town of Piedrahita.

The Piedrahita monastery was run by an order of Catholic friars called the Dominicans. Dominican friars tried to live by strict religious rules. And Tomás fit in well. He refused to use soft linen cloth. He wore only clothes made from rough animal hair. He lived in poverty. Tomás had money from his parents' estate. Yet he gave it all to the church.

The Dominicans had an important duty that must have been inspiring to Tomás. Since 1233, they had been in charge of the Inquisition. They traveled across Europe in hooded robes, searching for heretics. They used torture to get confessions. And their victims were often burned at the stake.

The judges, or inquisitors, would have said that they were doing God's work. In their view, Christians who did not follow the rules of the church spread evil across the land. In the battle against evil, no method was too harsh. The Dominicans did their job so fanatically that they were called the "Hounds of the Lord."

So far, the Inquisition had done almost nothing in Spain. But the Dominican "hounds" kept a close watch on the Spanish people. And Tomás de Torquemada was quickly becoming the most zealous hound of all.

Torquemada's fervor impressed his Dominican brothers. In 1452, they put the 32-year-old in charge of

31

the monastery of Santa Cruz, in the city of Segovia.

Torquemada took his place behind the walls of the monastery. Outside, life for Jews and conversos was getting more and more dangerous. In 1460, another preacher spread the gospel of hate. Alonso de Spina wrote a book attacking Jews and conversos. Then he went on the road to preach the old lies. Jews caused plagues, he claimed. They kidnapped Christian children and murdered them. Jewish doctors hid poison under their fingernails to kill their Christian patients. And conversos were no better, he said. They were not to be trusted. De Spina insisted it was time for the Inquisition to come to Spain.

De Spina's preaching helped revive prejudice against Jews. In 1468, it erupted in Segovia, Torquemada's new home. That spring, Christians in the city accused 15 innocent Jews of murder. Supposedly, the suspects had kidnapped a Christian child. On Good Friday, it was said, the Jews nailed the child to a cross. The local bishop put the suspects on trial. He found all 15 of them guilty.

IN THIS ART FROM 1474, Alonso de Spina (left), armed with a sword and an ax, tries to convert Jews while devils (bottom right) tempt his audience. Three people at the top left wear blindfolds because they "do not see the truth."

The entire incident was made up—a product of fear and prejudice. Still, many Christians—no doubt including Torquemada—were convinced that Jews and conversos were plotting against them.

But what could Torquemada do? He had little power. He wasn't well known outside the Dominican order. He had no influence over the laws of Spain. No king or queen came to seek his advice.

All of that was about to change.

CHAPTER 4

The Friar and the Princess

Torquemada makes
A POWERFUL FRIEND.

In 1467, WHILE TORQUEMADA WAS AT SANTA CRUZ, a 16-year-old princess was in Segovia. Isabella, princess of the kingdom of Castile, was well known around the city. She and her mother lived there at times during Isabella's childhood.

Isabella's mother wanted her to have a good Catholic education. Most likely, they showed up often at the Convent of Santa Cruz. According to at least

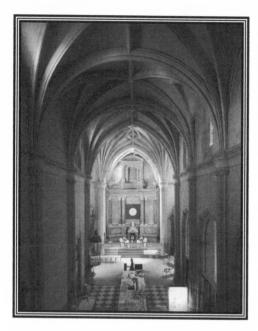

TORQUEMADA MET ISABELLA at the Convent of Santa Cruz. Its 800-year-old chapel still stands today in Segovia.

one writer, Torquemada became the princess' teacher.

Sometime in the next few years, Torquemada began hearing Isabella's confession. For Isabella, it was an important ritual. She probably met the friar in a chapel lit by candles. Torquemada sat hidden from view. Isabella confessed her sins to him. He offered her God's forgiveness in return.

According to one story, Torquemada got the

princess to make him a promise. He insisted that if she became queen, Isabella would devote her life to a single task. She would get rid of heresy in her kingdom.

Isabella was smart and stubborn. No one really knows if she made a promise to Torquemada. But she already had the determination it would take to become queen. In 1468, her half brother Henry IV was king of Castile. And he did not like his little half sister. He tried to choose a husband for Isabella. She refused, and in 1469, she made her own choice. Don Abraham Senior—one of the Jews who would later appeal to Isabella and Ferdinand for protection—helped arrange a marriage to Prince Ferdinand.

It was a wise choice. Ferdinand was next in line to become king of the neighboring kingdom of Aragon. The young couple could bring Spain's two largest kingdoms together.

Late in 1474, Isabella got what she wanted. Henry IV died. From Segovia, Isabella declared herself Queen of Castile. Torquemada stayed on as her confessor. In

FERDINAND HOPED to inherit the kingdom of Aragon
when his father, John II, died.

a matter of days, he had become one of the most
powerful men in Spain.

Just before Isabella became queen, Spain got a
warning of things to come. In 1473, Christians attacked
conversos in Córdoba. As in 1391, riots spread across the
land. In May 1474, the violence reached Segovia. Dead

ISABELLA FOLLOWED her half brother
Henry IV as ruler of Castile.

bodies piled up in the streets outside Torquemada's
monastery. Fortunately, the mayor stepped in to stop
the rioters. One witness said he acted just in time. If
the mayor had waited, all the conversos in Segovia
would have been killed.

The Inquisition Comes to Spain

Victory at Last

Torquemada gets the KING AND
QUEEN ON HIS SIDE.

FROM THE START, Torquemada was the queen's confessor. He quickly became one of her most trusted advisors. Finally, the zealous friar had the power to advance his plan. He insisted that Isabella launch the Inquisition.

But during the early years of her reign, Isabella wasn't interested. Jews and conversos, after all, held important positions in her court. Ferdinand had a Jewish doctor. The queen had three secretaries who were conversos. Abraham Senior was her chief tax collector. Isabella often stopped local officials from passing laws against Jews and conversos. One foreign visitor called her the "protector of the Jews."

Besides, Ferdinand and Isabella had more pressing problems. In 1475, Castile was in the midst of a civil war. After Henry IV's death, some powerful nobles refused to support Isabella.

Ferdinand and Isabella struggled to win control of Castile. The queen organized a royal police force. She seized thousands of acres of land from the rebellious nobles. She cracked down on crime. By 1477, the civil war was nearly under control.

Meanwhile, Torquemada continued to press for the Inquisition. That summer, he got help from the south.

In July 1477, Isabella moved her court to Seville. Seville and other southern cities had the largest Jewish and converso populations in all of Spain. They were also home to some of the most vicious preachers. One of them was a Dominican named Alonso de Hojeda.

As soon as the queen arrived, Hojeda began pushing for an Inquisition to investigate false Christians. Conversos, he argued, were all heretics. They were still secretly Jewish. They were traitors to Christian Spain. They were destroying the Church from the inside out.

Hojeda claimed he had evidence to back up his accusations. He filled Isabella's ears with stories about false Christians. One event supposedly took place around Easter in 1478. According to Hojeda, a young nobleman named Guzman sneaked out to visit his girlfriend. She lived with her wealthy converso family. When Guzman arrived, he found no sign of Easter. Instead, the family was preparing for the Jewish holiday of Passover.

Isabella listened to these tales for months. Finally, she formed a group of church officials to look into the accusations and prepare a report for her.

According to the officials' report, Hojeda was right. Many conversos secretly followed Jewish laws and practices. And the situation affected not only the south, but Castile and other areas as well. Secret Jews sat in positions of great power all over Spain. They supposedly tried to steer Catholics away from their faith. The country was in serious danger, the report claimed. Spain needed an Inquisition.

Isabella left Seville for Córdoba in the fall of 1478. When she saw Torquemada, he gave his full support to the report. Ferdinand, too, thought an Inquisition might help the crown. People who were found guilty of disobeying church law could be fined. Those executed would have all their property seized. The Spanish rulers were about to go to war against the Moors in Granada. They could use the extra funds.

Isabella was convinced. She sent an ambassador to Rome to meet with Pope Sixtus IV, the head of the Catholic Church. The ambassador told the pope that Ferdinand and Isabella wanted an Inquisition in Spain. And he insisted that the royal couple, not the

AS PRIEST AND CONFESSOR to the royal couple, Torquemada (left) had great influence over Ferdinand and Isabella.

Pope, have control over the inquisitors.

The Pope agreed. In November 1478, he wrote out the instructions. Ferdinand and Isabella could choose three church officials as inquisitors.

The inquisitors were given no power over Jews. Their job would be to go after heretics—

people who called themselves Christians but secretly refused to follow the rules of the Catholic Church. Conversos weren't the only heretics in Spain. But in Torquemada's view, they were the big danger. And from the beginning, they would be the Inquisition's main target.

In December, Torquemada left the court to go back to Segovia. He had work to do. A wealthy friend had died and left his fortune to the church. The friend wanted his money used to build a monastery at Ávila, a small town south of Segovia.

Torquemada made the 30-mile journey into the mountains from Segovia. It must have been a satisfying time for the 58-year-old friar. Here, he would build a house of God in the mountains.

Down below, in the valleys of Spain, a religious spirit was starting to spread, too. Spanish Christians had strayed from the faith too long, Torquemada felt. The country was finally getting ready to bring its people back to God. The Inquisition was coming to Spain.

CHAPTER 6

Seville Is Burning

The Inquisition begins its DIRTY WORK.

AFTER THE POPE'S ORDER, Spanish conversos had two more years of peace. Then, in 1480, the Inquisition began.

Isabella named Torquemada to her Royal Council, a group of her most powerful advisors. That September, she gave him the right to pick inquisitors. Ten days later, he selected two Dominican friars. Seville would be their first target.

In mid-October, the inquisitors arrived in Seville. They were met by their fellow Dominicans. In their black and white robes, they marched through the streets to the Convent of San Pablo. There, they set up their headquarters.

Seville was strangely quiet. In homes all across the city, conversos had been warned. Many of them guessed what was coming. Quickly, they packed as much as they could carry. In carts and on horseback, they left the city and fled to the countryside. They hid themselves on the estates of important nobles in the area.

Back in the city, the inquisitors were getting little help from city officials. For two months, it looked like a standoff. Then, Torquemada got Isabella to act. On December 27, she ordered the city officials to help the inquisitors. A week later, the inquisitors gathered in the city's cathedral. They read an order to the great nobles around Seville. The nobles were to seize all the people hiding on their estates and turn them in.

The nobles of Seville must have been shocked

by the order. These men ruled their own lands. They collected their own taxes. They often resisted the orders of kings. Now, two friars—with support from the queen—were telling them what to do.

Within two weeks, the nobles gave in. Hundreds of conversos were led back to Seville in chains. Before long, the Convent of San Pablo overflowed with prisoners. They soon were moved to a castle nearby.

After their first success, the inquisitors read another order. They demanded that the people of Seville report anyone they suspected of heresy. In case people needed help, they published a list written by Torquemada. It offered 37 ways to recognize a heretic. Anyone who broke church rules and ate meat during the Catholic holiday of Lent was a suspect. So were people who didn't go to confession. Anyone who followed Jewish customs should be immediately turned in.

By then, Torquemada had begun to develop a

network of spies. Some of them were paid to inform on their neighbors. Others did so out of fear. Still others simply believed they were doing God's work. One eager young priest climbed to the roof of San Pablo every Saturday. He looked for chimneys that weren't producing smoke. The people inside, he assumed, were obeying Jewish law by refusing to light fires on the Jewish Sabbath. He had them arrested and handed over to the inquisitors.

By February, the fanatical laws of the Inquisition had taken over Seville. Guards stood watch over the gates of the city to keep conversos from leaving. Prisoners arrived by the hundreds.

According to one story, the inquisitors helped their own cause by claiming that they had uncovered a plot. A wealthy converso named Diego de Susan had supposedly gathered friends in the church of San Salvador. The friends each agreed to collect weapons. When the time was right, they would kill the inquisitors.

If the plan existed, it never got started. The inquisitors arrested de Susan and his friends. They were all found guilty of heresy.

On February 6, 1481, the Inquisition took its first

THE INQUISITION BURNED its victims in public. This man's crime? He vandalized an image of the Virgin Mary.

victims. A crowd gathered in the streets of Seville. The inquisitors marched six prisoners from the castle to the cathedral. There, the prisoners listened to a long sermon by Alonso de Hojeda, the Dominican who had encouraged Ferdinand and Isabella to start the Inquisition. Then they were sent to a field outside of town. Guards tied the prisoners to six stakes. They lit a pile of dry wood under each one. The people of Seville watched while the prisoners slowly burned to death.

Several days after the first burnings, Alonso de Hojeda got sick. Terrible sores opened wounds in his skin. His lungs filled with fluid. Within days, he was dead.

The plague had returned to Seville.

But even the Black Death failed to slow the Inquisition. The inquisitors built a huge stone platform for the burnings. It was used in February and again in March.

By this time, the plague was killing people faster than the Inquisition. Conversos pleaded with the

A PRIEST BLESSES MONKS infected with the plague.
Some people blamed Jews for spreading the disease,
but Jews died at just as high a rate as everyone else.

city's mayor to let them leave the disease-filled city. He agreed, and thousands of people fled into the countryside.

The inquisitors, too, left to save their lives. But they continued their relentless search for false Christians. In the nearby town of Aracena, they burned 23 people. They also judged a number of dead people guilty of heresy. The victims' bones were dug up and thrown in the fire.

When the plague disappeared, the inquisitors returned to Seville. They continued prosecuting and punishing those they decided were heretics. In November, a witness counted up their victims. In its first year, the Spanish Inquisition had burned 298 people. It sent 79 more to prison for life. Together with the plague, the Inquisition had nearly destroyed one of Spain's most lively cities.

BLAMING THE VICTIMS

MORE THAN 70 YEARS before Torquemada's birth, a strange and violent disease attacked Europe. It came in the fall of 1347. Its first symptom was a headache. Soon, its victims began to stagger. By the third day, swollen lumps appeared in the armpits or the groin. The heart beat wildly, trying to pump blood to dying tissue. Black spots appeared on the skin from internal bleeding. And by the fifth day, nearly all victims were dead.

The bubonic plague—also known as the Black Death—had arrived. In five years, it killed off one-third of the population of Europe.

No one had any idea what caused the plague. But many of its victims wanted someone to blame.

The Jews became their scapegoat. Jews were accused of spreading the disease by poisoning wells. One by one, cities and towns all across Europe expelled Jews—or worse. By the time the disease passed, Jews in 200 towns had been butchered or burned. The plague returned from time to time. And each time it brought danger for the Jews of Europe.

CHAPTER 7

Grand Inquisitor

After a fight with the Pope,
TORQUEMADA IS IN CHARGE.

AT THE END OF 1481, Torquemada must have been pleased. The Inquisition had punished hundreds of so-called heretics. Thousands more had fled overseas or gone into hiding. The results seemed to prove what he and Hojeda had believed all along. The Spanish Church was full of traitors. Finally, Torquemada had them on the run.

While conversos in Seville feared for their lives, Ferdinand and Isabella went on a tour of Castile and Aragon. They, too, must have been pleased. In 1479, the civil war in Castile had ended for good. And in Aragon, Ferdinand had become king after the death of his father. Most of Spain was now united in the hands of the royal couple.

As they traveled, Ferdinand and Isabella heard reports about the inquisitors in Seville. When they returned, they met with Torquemada. Together they decided that Seville was just the beginning. Ferdinand began naming inquisitors for Aragon. He also got the Pope to approve seven more inquisitors for Castile. Torquemada was one of them.

However, in Rome, the Pope had his concerns about events in Spain. For a year, Spanish conversos had been fleeing for their lives. Many of them made the 1,000-mile trip to Rome. They arrived with stories from Seville. The inquisitors were out of control, they said. They were burning good Christians to death.

Pope Sixtus IV may have been shocked at the injustices. He may also have seen a chance to increase his wealth. He listened to each converso's story. He collected a sum of money. Then he gave out pardons. The conversos could return to Spain with a letter of protection from the Pope.

In April 1482, Jews and conversos all across Spain got a ray of hope from Rome. The Pope decided to challenge Ferdinand and Isabella. He wrote an order charging the Inquisition with great crimes. The

POPE SIXTUS IV gave his approval to the Inquisition in Spain, then objected to its methods.

inquisitors didn't care about saving souls, he claimed. They wanted only wealth. They found people guilty without proof. They set a bad example and caused "disgust to many."

The Pope demanded rights for those accused of heresy. They must be told the names of their accusers. They must be given a lawyer. And finally, they must be allowed to seek pardons from the Pope.

The ray of hope didn't last long. Ferdinand wrote to the Pope in May. He could not believe that the Pope had given the order, he said. Surely the Pope had been fooled by clever conversos trying to escape punishment for their crimes. The rules would ruin the Inquisition in Spain, Ferdinand insisted. Then he ended by vowing, "I intend never to let them take effect."

These letters started a long battle for control over the Inquisition. But Ferdinand had won the first round. The Pope had no real power over the Spanish king. In October Sixtus IV canceled his order.

The next year, Ferdinand and Isabella created a Supreme Council to oversee the Inquisition. The council needed a strong leader. It needed someone to hire and fire inquisitors. It needed a man who would stop at nothing to protect the Spanish Church from all threats—real or imagined.

That man was Tomás de Torquemada. In October 1483, the Pope agreed to make him Spain's first Grand Inquisitor. Over the next few years, he would extend the long arm of the Inquisition into every corner of Spain.

The news sent a shiver of fear through Jewish and converso homes.

Tomás de Torquemada in Pictures

SCHOOL DAYS

Tomás studied at the convent of San Pablo, a Dominican school in Valladolid. The church of San Pablo still stands today.

HARD LESSONS

Dominican friars were dedicated to education and to preaching the gospel. Young men like Tomás had to study hard to become part of the order.

FUTURE QUEEN
Isabella probably met
Torquemada at the
Monastery of Santa
Cruz when she was
just a teenager.

POWER PLAY

When Isabella became queen of Castile, Torquemada (left) was her
confessor. When it came to religious matters, he held great influence
over both Isabella and Ferdinand.

AUDIENCE WITH THE POPE

Torquemada (right) examines Pope Sixtus IV's order naming him the head of the Inquisition in Spain.

THIRD DEGREE

Torquemada's inquisitors questioned their prisoners without telling them what they were accused of.

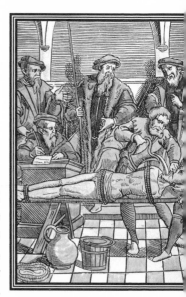

WATER TORTURE

Prisoners who refused to confess were often forced to suffer through treatments like the *toca*, or water torture. This torture involved forcing water down the prisoner's throat.

FEAR TACTICS

The *garrucha*, or pulley, could pull a prisoner's arms and legs from their sockets.

BURNED AT THE STAKE

Heretics who did not apologize for their supposed crimes got the ultimate punishment. They were burned to death in a public ceremony.

RUMOR MILL

These men were accused of trying to turn communion wafers into a magic potion. These Jews and conversos were also said to have killed a child. The charges were totally untrue. But the men were found guilty and killed.

A FINAL PLEA

Jewish leaders tried to keep Ferdinand and Isabella from expelling the Jews from Spain, while Torquemada (in black cape) urged the king and queen not to change their minds.

EXILED

Isaac Abravanel was an important financier for the Spanish court. After 1492, he wandered homeless, like the rest of Spain's Jews.

A PLACE IN HISTORY

Torquemada had this painting of St. Peter, one of the founders of the Christian church, done for his monastery in Ávila. The Grand Inquisitor had himself (lower left) painted into the scene.

PART 3

Reign of Terror

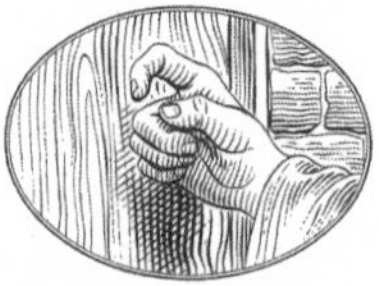

CHAPTER 8

The Arrival

THE INQUISITORS spread their influence—and terror—across Spain.

UNDER TORQUEMADA'S DIRECTION, the Inquisition spread across Spain like the plague. Inquisitors went to Córdoba and Jaén in the south. They traveled to Ciudad Real, Valladolid, Segovia, and Ávila in the north. In Aragon, they began their cruel work in Valencia, Barcelona, and Saragossa. There were wandering courts, or tribunals, as well. With a small army of guards, the wandering inquisitors traveled wherever they sensed opportunities. Torquemada himself often joined them.

By 1485, each inquisitor traveled with a handwritten document. On it were the rules of the Inquisition, written by Torquemada. These rules shaped the spread of terror across the land.

The Inquisition began in much the same way everywhere. The inquisitors arrived with several aides. They rode into town with an armed guard drawn from the families of local nobles. They set up offices in a Dominican monastery. Often, they moved into castles with prisons big enough for the job before them.

The inquisitors then chose a Sunday to announce their purpose. They ordered all the people of the city to gather at the cathedral. The head inquisitor or a local priest preached a sermon. He read a long list of heresies. Then he demanded that all heretics confess their crimes.

The inquisitor gave everyone a "period of grace." If people came in within 40 days and confessed, they would be treated well. They would pay a fine. They might be banned from holding public office. They would have to give up wearing silk or jewelry. They would then be considered "reconciled," or forgiven. By this time, they had been publicly shamed. But they escaped with their lives and most of their property.

In addition, all citizens had to swear upon the Bible and a cross that they would turn in anyone they suspected of heresy. They had 60 days to expose their friends and family. After that, they could be found guilty of aiding heresy. For that, they would be burned at the stake.

After the sermon, the inquisitors nailed their announcement to the wall of the cathedral for all to see.

There it stood, a single piece of paper on the wall of a church. It must have created great fear as people filed by to read it. What were they to do? In many converso families, people still observed Jewish customs. Would their family members turn them in? Or would they stay silent and risk a terrible death?

HOPING FOR MERCY, a man confesses to an inquisitor in Toledo.

Even sons and daughters as young as 14 were expected to testify against their parents.

In most cities, people flooded in to confess during the period of grace. In a single year in Toledo, 2,500 turned themselves in. A woman named Beatriz Gonzalez admitted that she said prayers on the Jewish holiday of Yom Kippur. Maria Diaz lit candles early on the sabbath. Constanza Nuñez gave oil to the Jewish temple to keep its flame lit.

Witnesses, too, came forward by the hundreds to accuse others of heresy. No one knew what their friends or enemies might say about them. Each witness gave his information in secret. That made it easy to lie.

Witnesses probably accused hundreds of faithful Catholics. Some of them told lies to hurt their enemies. Others would do anything to please the inquisitors. Often, witnesses dug up information from long ago. In 1483, Juan de Chinchilla was sent to his death for things that had happened 20 years earlier. In the case of Sancho de Ciudad, one witness told about an event that had happened 40 years before.

In 1485, Torquemada insisted that Jews be questioned as well. He had the inquisitors in Toledo bring all rabbis in for interrogation. Did any conversos appear in synagogue? Which ones visited the ghetto? If the Jewish leaders refused to answer, they, too, could be put to death.

Under these conditions, even people who had not broken any laws confessed—just in case. After all, they had no idea what information the inquisitors were digging up. If they failed to confess, they could be put to death.

A resident of Sigüenza wondered how many false confessions the inquisitors collected. "Who is there who has not gone to be reconciled out of fear, even though he has done nothing?"

C H A P T E R   9

The Interrogation

The inquisitors find ways to
MAKE PEOPLE TALK.

FOR 40 DAYS, the inquisitors gathered their so-called evidence. People sneaked in to confess their crimes. Witnesses turned in friends and family members. Neighbors eyed each other, wondering whom they could trust. Here and there, people were arrested. But under Torquemada's rules, inquisitors were supposed to examine the evidence first. In the meantime, entire cities waited in suspense.

Finally, the period of grace ended. The inquisitors met to review each case. Then they made arrests.

Guards appeared at doorsteps. Suspects were led off in the middle of dinner. They disappeared into the prisons of the Inquisition.

Guards returned quickly to each suspect's house. With them came a secretary. The secretary carefully noted every piece of property. Then the Inquisition took control of it all. Piece by piece, everything a suspect owned would be sold to support his or her family while the case went to trial.

For most suspects, the trial was a long nightmare. It began in jail. For weeks, they sat in a damp, dark cell. Three times, an inquisitor appeared at the door and ordered the suspects to confess. "Look into your soul," the inquisitor might say. "Confess your crime. God will have mercy on you." Not once would the inquisitor mention what the charges were.

Every prisoner had the same problem. To save their own lives, they had to guess—and confess to—the charges that had been brought against them. If they guessed correctly and confessed fully, they could not be put to death. If they convinced the inquisitors that they were truly sorry, they might even escape with their property. But if their confession failed to match the charges against them, they were in trouble. They could be considered liars and burned at the stake.

After the inquisitor's third visit, the questioning began. Suspects were led to a large room lit by candles. Four men sat at a table. One was a secretary, who would take detailed notes. Another was the prosecutor. The third was often a priest. The fourth was clearly the most important person at the table. He was the inquisitor. In important cases, it might be Torquemada himself.

The prisoner sat, usually alone. Suspects had the right to use a lawyer. But few lawyers were willing to defend people accused of heresy.

On the table stood a tall cross and a Bible. For a time there was nothing but silence. The inquisitor shuffled papers. The prisoner could only guess what the inquisitors knew—or suspected. Finally, the prisoner was asked to place his hand on the Bible and swear to tell the truth.

The questioning began: Did the prisoner know why he was arrested? Wouldn't he like to confess now and get it over with? It would please God. And the inquisitors would be able to show mercy.

SUSPECTS FACED THEIR INTERROGATORS
without knowing what they were accused of. The process
was designed to leave victims scared and confused.

If the suspect refused to confess, he was hit with a quick string of questions. Did he know any heretics? How often did he go to confession? Who was his confessor? How often did he pray?

Suspects were trapped. If they hadn't broken any church laws, they could simply tell the truth. But if witnesses had told lies about them, they could still be found guilty. And guilt without a confession led to death. What's more, the list of heresies was long—and many people had slipped at some point in their past.

Under this kind of pressure, it was easy to break down. Many suspects confessed to anything. Others fumbled their way through the answers. But they had to be careful. The inquisitors listened closely for contradictions. If they thought a suspect was lying, they might consider the next step. They had only to look at Torquemada's instructions.

It was written in Article XV: If the crime is "half-proven," the inquisitors may put "the accused to the torture."

CHAPTER 10

Feet to the Fire

Some suspects are subjected to
TERRIBLE TORTURES.

ALL SUSPECTS QUESTIONED by the Inquisition
had one great fear. They knew they could be tortured.
Most people escaped without being led to the dark rooms
of the torture chamber. But the threat was always
there. It was usually enough to make a suspect
confess to anything.

Torquemada sometimes oversaw torture sessions
personally. And the process was terrifying. Every
suspect was taken slowly through several steps. At
every step, they were urged to confess.

The process began with threats. If the threats didn't work, guards led the prisoner to a darkened room, perhaps in the dungeon of a castle. In the room, the inquisitor sat in a grand chair. A representative of the bishop was there, too. A guard in a black mask stood ready to do his work. A secretary sat at a table. He would write down every word spoken during the session. A doctor might be there as well, in case his services were needed.

The people in the room, however, didn't hold the prisoner's attention for long. Not far away stood the instruments of torture. There were many devices available. But the inquisitors had their favorites. There was the *garrucha*, the *toca*, and the *potro*.

The *garrucha*, or pulley, hung from the ceiling. A prisoner could easily imagine it in operation. He would be tied at the wrists, a heavy weight hanging from the ankles. The guard would raise him slowly into the air, then let him fall with a jerk. The limbs might survive one or two jolts. Before long, they would be pulled from their sockets.

Next came the *toca*, a kind of water torture. It was more complicated than the *garrucha*, and just as frightening. The suspect would be strapped to a table, head tilted down. Wooden sticks clogged the nostrils. An iron clamp held the mouth open. A guard stuffed a linen cloth in the mouth and poured water onto it. The gagging and choking began. The torture was stopped only to allow the suspect a chance to confess.

THE THREAT OF TORTURE led many people
to confess to things they hadn't done.

Finally, there was the *potro*, where tight cords bound arms, legs and waist to a rack. The guard controlled the tension on the cords. A few twists and they bit into flesh. A few more, and the blood stopped flowing. Arms turned blue. Pain shot through the body. Then the cords were loosened for another chance to confess—before they were tightened once again.

There were other methods as well. Prisoners were whipped. They were hung by their thumbs until blood flowed from their nails. They were strapped to a chair with grease on their feet and cooked slowly over a fire.

After viewing all the ways they could be tortured, prisoners were stripped naked. Next they were tied to one of the torture devices. Finally, if they still hadn't confessed, the torture began.

Few records from Torquemada's time still survive. But later accounts give us a look inside the torture chamber. In 1568, inquisitors tortured a woman accused of secretly following Jewish law. A secretary took notes while the woman pleaded for mercy.

First, the inquisitors ordered her to be placed on the *potro*.

"Señores," she pleaded, "why will you not tell me what I have to say?"

The guard began to lift her onto the table. "Señor, put me on the ground," she begged.

The inquisitors insisted that she tell them what she had done wrong. "I don't remember," she said. "Take me away. I did what the witnesses say."

Twice more the inquisitor demanded that she tell him what the witnesses had accused her of. Twice she said she did not know. Finally, the inquisitor ordered the cords to be tightened.

"Señor, do you not see how these people are killing me?" she pleaded. "I did it—for God's sake let me go!"

CHAPTER 11

Fires of Hell

Some suspects are publicly punished;
OTHERS ARE BURNED
TO DEATH.

BITTER COLD CAME TO THE CITY of Toledo on the morning of February 12, 1486. Yet the people didn't seem to care. Huge crowds gathered in the streets. They had come from miles around to see the results of the Inquisition's work. One of the people in the crowd that day, a man named Sebastian de Orozco, described the scene in detail.

A somber parade made its way through the city. A section of Familiars—the guards of the Inquisition—

led the parade. They walked slowly, two by two. Behind them stretched a long column of penitents. The penitents were prisoners who had confessed that they had broken church laws. There were 750 in all. Now, it was time for them to repent. They were ready to admit their crime in public and promise to obey the church in the future.

CONVICTED HERETICS were forced to parade through town wearing bright yellow shirts called *sanbenitos*. Later, priests hung the shirts in church as a reminder of the penitents' crimes.

The penitents included many of Toledo's important citizens. They shuffled along in two groups. Women were separated from men. Each person wore a long yellow shirt called a *sanbenito*. Underneath, they were naked. Often, the penitents were forced to walk barefoot on the frozen ground. In their hands, they carried unlit candles. When they were fully reconciled to the church, the candles would be lit again.

The long line of people finally arrived at the cathedral. Two church officials met the penitents at the door. With their thumbs they made the sign of the cross near each person's forehead. Each time, they spoke the same words: "Receive the Sign of the Cross which you denied."

Inside the cathedral, a large platform had been built. On it sat the inquisitors. Slowly, the cathedral filled with people. A priest preached a sermon. Then a secretary stood. One by one, he called the names of the penitents. And one by one he read lists of their crimes.

The inquisitors sat in silence while the punishments were announced. No penitent could hold public office. None could wear jewelry or silk. Each would be fined one-fifth of their property. The money would go directly to the war against the Moors. Finally, the

PENITENTS IN POINTED CAPS and *sanbenitos* are sentenced in a cathedral. This painting, *Inquisition Scene*, is by the famous Spanish artist Francisco de Goya.

penitents were told to gather every Friday for six weeks. They would be marched through the streets, naked from the waist up. As they walked they were to whip themselves with cords of rope.

The penitents were then warned not to go back to their old ways. If they did, they would be burned at the stake.

The ceremony was over by 2 P.M. The people of Toledo went back to their homes for the midday meal. They came back for more in April. Another 900 penitents were reconciled then. In June, the inquisitors dealt with 750 more.

The scene was repeated all across Spain. The ceremony was called an *auto-da-fé*, or act of faith. It was Torquemada's grand performance. Every *auto-da-fé* announced the work of the Inquisition in public. It forced the victims to admit their so-called crimes to their neighbors. And it sent a message to the Christians of Spain: Follow the laws of the church—or else.

But so far, the *autos-da-fé* in Toledo had not included

the Inquisition's most terrifying punishment. Its victims had merely been humiliated in public. In August, however, the accused who still hadn't confessed would be killed.

On August 16, 1486, 25 prisoners awoke in Toledo to the last day of their lives. At 6 A.M., guards led the 20 men and five women up from the prison. Their hands were tied with ropes that looped around their necks. All 25 wore *sanbenitos*. On them, someone had painted bright red images of dragons and devils.

Like the penitents in February, the prisoners were led to the cathedral. But the parade looked somewhat different. Two Dominican friars walked alongside each prisoner. The friars asked the prisoners again and again if they were ready to confess. In the eyes of the friars, the question was extremely important. People who confessed before their execution would die as Christians. They would escape the fires of hell and live forever in heaven.

In addition, those who confessed would receive what the church considered an act of mercy. They would be strangled to death before the fires were lit.

Behind the prisoners came a group of men carrying long green poles. Strange-looking figures stuffed with

AS A WARNING to other Christians, *autos-da-fé* took place in public. In the background of this scene, nine heretics are already burning at the stake.

straw dangled from the poles. The figures, called effigies, represented people who had gone into hiding and escaped the Inquisition. The effigies were headed for the fires as well.

By this time, the chilling ceremony at the cathedral was familiar to the people of Toledo. They heard a sermon. Then each prisoner sat on a stool in the hot sun. The secretary read a list of crimes. One by one, the prisoners were handed over to the city's armed guards. They were placed on donkeys and led off to the burning place. In Toledo, it was called *La Dehesa*. In the field stood a white cross and 25 stakes. Guards tied the prisoners to the stakes. The fires were lit. Those who confessed were immediately strangled. The rest died slowly in the flames.

PART 4

Exile!

CHAPTER 12

Aragon Resists

A few rebels try—in vain—to
OPPOSE THE INQUISITION.

IN CASTILE, THE BURNINGS CONTINUED. Three more victims went up in flames in Toledo the day after the 25 were burned. In two years in Ciudad Real, 52 died at the stake. In 1485, 53 were killed in Guadalupe. In city after city, the story was the same.

In a few places there were signs of protest. Some conversos in Toledo supposedly planned to kill the inquisitors and take over the city. The story was probably invented to justify the burnings.

Torquemada's hometown of Segovia showed signs of revolt. The converso bishop there refused to allow inquisitors into the city. Torquemada responded by charging the bishop's parents with heresy. When the bishop left for Rome, to complain to the Pope, the inquisitors got their start.

Most Castilians, however, felt powerless to resist. In most places, Torquemada's Inquisition took over without opposition.

The region of Aragon proved to be a different story. Torquemada made his first trip there in April 1484. Local officials made it clear that he was not welcome. Five of Aragon's most important leaders at the time were conversos. Some of them refused to meet with the fanatical Grand Inquisitor.

Torquemada appointed two inquisitors for Aragon, Gaspar Juglar and Pedro Arbués de Epila. He left in May, and the inquisitors set up headquarters in the city of Saragossa. Brave city officials protested to the king. The people of Aragon were good Christians, they said. Ferdinand quickly sent a letter back. He turned their protest into a sign of guilt. "If there are so few heretics," he wrote, "there should not be such [fear] of the Inquisition."

Arbués and Juglar sent two inquisitors to the town of Teruel. They found the gates locked when they arrived. The city leaders wrote to the Pope and to Ferdinand. "This is a kingdom of Christians," they insisted. In response, Ferdinand raised an army to attack Teruel. The city held out until the spring of 1485. Finally, it was forced to open its doors to the inquisitors.

That fall, the Inquisition met its most serious challenge. It happened in Saragossa. On September 15, the inquisitor Arbués entered the city's cathedral to pray. He knew he had enemies everywhere. As usual, he wore a steel cap and a coat of armor for protection. He knelt at the altar and bowed his head.

While Arbués prayed, eight men crept out of the shadows. They sneaked up behind Arbués. One of them raised a sword. He swung at the inquisitor's back. The sword sliced between the armor and the helmet, wounding Arbués in the neck. Arbués got up and staggered down the aisle. Another man wounded him on the arm. A third drove a knife into his body. Arbués collapsed on the spot and died two days later.

The assassins may have felt they had won a great victory. If so, the feeling didn't last long. Public opinion turned against the murderers. People called Arbués a hero and claimed that miracles happened at his death. The bell in the cathedral rang all by itself, they said. His blood dried on the cathedral steps and then turned to liquid again.

The Christians of Saragossa turned against their neighbors. Mobs filled the streets, looking for Jews and conversos. The archbishop of Saragossa rode through the streets to quiet the crowd. The Inquisition would find and punish the murderers, he promised.

Torquemada made sure the promise was fulfilled. He named new inquisitors for Aragon. Over the next year and a half, the inquisitors held more than 14 *autos-da-fé* in the city. Forty-two people were burned at the stake.

One by one, the assassins confessed in public. But their confessions got them no mercy. The hands of one of Arbués's killers were cut off and nailed to the doors of a public building. The man was then beheaded and cut into quarters. His body parts were displayed in public for all to see. Another prisoner decided to finish the job himself. He killed himself in prison by eating pieces of a glass lamp.

By 1487, all signs of revolt in Saragossa were gone.

CHAPTER 13

The Final Nail

A STRANGE SCANDAL helps
Torquemada's campaign against the Jews.

THE VIOLENCE IN SARAGOSSA may have made Torquemada fear for his own safety. He knew the Inquisition had plenty of enemies. After Arbués was killed, Torquemada lived in fear of assassination. He often traveled with 250 bodyguards.

But Torquemada was also reaching the height of his power. In Segovia, he ruled over an important Dominican monastery. In Ávila, he oversaw the building of a new one. At the Spanish Court, he was Isabella's most trusted advisor.

The queen often insisted that Torquemada accompany her as she followed the progress of the war in Granada. In August 1487, he was there when the Spanish army retook Málaga, an important port city in Granada. He supposedly told Ferdinand and Isabella to kill all the Moors in the city. The king and queen decided not to follow his advice. But they did burn several conversos.

Few people were safe from Torquemada's fanaticism—no matter how powerful they might be. In April 1491, Torquemada even had Ferdinand's secretary, Luis de Santangel, arrested. Luis came from a powerful converso family in Aragon. Many of his relatives had been found guilty in the Arbués assassination. Luis was forced to parade through the streets in a *sanbenito*.

But no matter how far Torquemada's influence reached, he still wanted more power. He wanted to extend the reach of the Inquisition. And Jews who had never converted were his next targets. He was convinced that they tempted conversos back into their old ways. If the Jews were gone, he believed, conversos would be less likely to backslide.

On a small scale, Torquemada had already tried a solution. In 1483, he ordered the Jews banned from the cities of Seville, Córdoba, and Cádiz. In 1486, they were ordered out of Saragossa, Albarracín, and Teruel. But the orders were not enforced. And Jews who left one Spanish city could simply settle in another.

Torquemada wanted a permanent solution. He wanted all the Jews in Spain expelled. But Ferdinand and Isabella weren't ready to go that far. Jews were an important part of the economy in Spain. Abraham Senior was in charge of all tax collectors for Castile. Isaac Abravanel collected the tax on sheep. A Jew named David Abulafia organized supplies for the troops in Granada. Spanish Jews often appealed to the king and queen for protection. Isabella felt she had a duty to respond. "All the Jews in my realms," she wrote, "are under my help and protection."

But conditions were changing fast. The war in

Granada was almost over. Ferdinand and Isabella would take over a rich new land. Perhaps they could do without the wealth of the Jews.

Then in the summer of 1490, a strange scandal gave Torquemada the ammunition he needed to convince the royal couple to expel the Jews.

That June, a converso named Benito Garcia spent the night in a tavern in Astorga. Some drunks opened his traveling bag. Inside, they supposedly found a wafer stolen from a Church service. The wafer was an important part of the communion ritual, and it was a crime to steal one. The men turned Garcia in. Local officials gave him 200 lashes, the water torture, and the *potro*.

Before long, Garcia admitted that he was a secret Jew. It's not clear what else he confessed. But by August, seven more people had been arrested—five conversos and two Jews.

Torquemada began to give the case his personal attention. He had the prisoners transferred to Segovia, where he could watch over them. In the fall, he had them moved to Ávila.

In December, a young Jewish cobbler named Yucé Franco went on trial. The ridiculous charges against him sound today like the plot of a bad horror film. Franco, Garcia, and the other prisoners were accused of murdering a Christian boy to make a magic potion. They had supposedly mixed the child's heart with the communion wafer. The result was a spell that would make Christians go mad and die.

Franco told the inquisitors the story was "the greatest falsehood in the world."

But seven months later, he began to confess. With help from the *potro*, the inquisitors put together a bizarre fiction. The prisoners supposedly nailed the child to a cross. A rabbi named Tazarte supposedly cut out the heart. He brought it to a cave near the village of La Guardia. With a few magic words, everyone in the cave would be protected forever from the Inquisition.

On November 16, 1491, the eight prisoners left Torquemada's monastery at Ávila. Guards led them up the hill to town. The inquisitors read the details of the crime aloud for all to hear. The prisoners were then tied to the stake and burned to death. Yucé Franco and another Jew had their flesh torn with hot irons before the fires were lit.

The preposterous story of the "Holy Child of La Guardia" spread quickly. No Christian child had actually been reported missing. No body had been found. But that didn't seem to matter. The inquisitors sent copies of the sentence to churches across Spain. Preachers read the story aloud. And once again, violence broke out. A Jew was stoned to death in Ávila. Mobs gathered outside the ghettos in other cities. On December 16, Ferdinand wrote an order from Córdoba. No Jews were to be harmed.

Eight months later, a mob would have a hard time finding a Jew anywhere in Spain.

CHAPTER 14

Exodus

The Jews are
FORCED OUT OF SPAIN.

ON JANUARY 2, 1492, Torquemada stood behind Isabella in Granada. He watched as the Moorish King Abdallah surrendered to the Catholic queen. The war was finally over. The last Muslim ruler in Western Europe had been defeated.

Ferdinand and Isabella dealt kindly with Muslims— at least at first. The people of Granada were free to "live in their own religion." No one had to join the Catholic faith. No mosques would be torn down. All Christians had to ask permission to enter Muslim holy sites.

THE LAST MUSLIM RULER of Granada surrendered to Ferdinand and Isabella in the Alhambra Palace during the early days of 1492.

Then the Spanish rulers turned their attention to the Jews. Don Isaac and Don Abraham made their final plea. And the decision was made.

On March 31, 1492, Ferdinand and Isabella turned their backs on the Jews of Spain. They gave the order. And they did it in language that could have been crafted by Torquemada.

For 12 years, Ferdinand and Isabella wrote, the laws of Castile had tried to separate Jews and Christians. The Inquisition had tried to keep conversos from sliding into heresy. But the Jews continued to "steal faithful Christians from our holy Catholic faith," the order said. They continued to attract Christians to "their evil beliefs." They continued to commit "the greatest, most dangerous, and most contagious of crimes." For these reasons, the Spanish rulers commanded all Jews "to leave our kingdoms and never to return to them."

History has no record of Torquemada's reaction. But the Grand Inquisitor must have taken pleasure in this injustice. He had devoted his life to bringing all Spaniards into the Catholic Church. Now, he seemed to have won.

As for the Jews, their lives were thrown into chaos. The order gave them four months to make a decision. They could convert to Christianity or leave the country. If they left, they could not bring gold or silver with them. Those who returned after leaving would be put to death. Any Christians caught helping a Jew after July 31 would lose all their property.

All across Spain, Jews tried to settle their affairs. Don Isaac traveled the country to collect debts for his friends. People tried desperately to sell their land. Most took whatever they could get. One man might sell a house for a donkey. Another might let a vineyard go for a roll of cloth.

Slowly, the Jews gathered what they could and left Spain. Some crossed into Portugal on foot. Others headed for port cities. They boarded overcrowded boats bound for Pisa or Naples. At the dock, they had to pay a tax to Spain before they could leave.

By the time they arrived in Italy, they were thin and tired. They looked like "dead men," according to a diplomat who watched the boats dock in Genoa. "No one could witness the sufferings of the Jews without being moved," he said.

Many Jews chose to convert so they could stay in Spain. Don Abraham Senior was one of them. For decades he had served the crown as a Jew. Now, at age 80, he let himself be baptized. About half the Jews in Spain did the same.

Don Isaac Abravanel refused to follow his friend. He was deeply devoted to Judaism. He was not going to desert his faith.

Before the deadline, Don Isaac heard a rumor that Christians were plotting to kidnap his grandson. The plotters wanted to baptize the boy. They hoped to force the Abravanels to stay in Spain with their fortune. Don Isaac had the boy sent to Portugal to protect him.

Then Don Isaac returned to the sad job at hand. He did what he could to help people leave. Finally, he boarded a boat for Italy. There, just four years later, he found out that his grandson had been forced to convert in Portugal.

It's unclear how many Jews were forced out of Spain. Don Isaac claimed that "three hundred thousand people left on foot from all the provinces of the king." Most likely the number was around 100,000. Many of them lived in poverty in other parts of Europe. Those who moved to Portugal were kicked out in 1496.

Some Jews were welcomed into the Ottoman Empire, which was ruled by Muslims. The sultan, Bayezid II, was the ruler of the empire. He said he was amazed at the King of Spain. Ferdinand had given the Ottomans his best people.

THE CHRISTIAN RULERS of Spain look down on a family of Jews left homeless by the expulsion order. The man in the robe with the long white beard is probably meant to be Torquemada.

THE OCEAN BLUE

ON JULY 31, 1492, THE LAST OF THE JEWS LEFT SPAIN. Three days later, three more ships left the Spanish port of Palos. They headed west into the Atlantic Ocean, looking for a sea route to Asia. The commander of the voyage was Christopher Columbus.

After ten weeks at sea, Columbus became the first European to set foot in the New World. He brought the spirit of the Inquisition with him.

After his first voyage, Columbus warned Ferdinand and Isabella to allow only "Christian Catholics" in the New World.

Of course, the "new" world was already filled with millions of Native Americans. None of them had ever heard of Christianity. What was to be done with them?

On Columbus's second voyage, five priests went with him. They had instructions from the Spanish rulers. They were to "win over" the Indians "to our Holy Catholic Faith." Indians who converted would be protected by Spanish law. Those who did not were left to fend for themselves. Most of them became slaves.

CHAPTER 15

Final Years

The fanatic inquisitor
LIVES TO A RIPE OLD AGE.

By THE END OF 1492, the Grand Inquisitor had executed his plan. He could stand in Ávila and look out over a land ruled solely by Christians. Even the monastery itself was a symbol of his career. The land beneath it had once been a Jewish cemetery. Builders destroyed the cemetery to make room for Torquemada's monastery.

At 72, Torquemada was an old man. In the 1400s, few people lived that long. He was beginning to show the strain of his years. A disease called gout was taking over his body. His joints swelled. It hurt to walk around.

Tired and in pain, Torquemada retired as confessor to the king and queen. He moved to Ávila. From the monastery he fought to keep control over the Inquisition. Pope Alexander VI worried—wisely—that Torquemada was ruining the reputation of the church. In 1494, Alexander made Torquemada share his power with three other inquisitors.

Not surprisingly, Torquemada worked with cold determination until his last day. Under his watchful eye, the Inquisition burned 127 people in Ávila between 1492 and 1498. In 1498, he sent a secret messenger to King Henry VII of England. Torquemada wanted England to punish anyone trying to escape from the Inquisition. Apparently, Henry agreed. According to the messenger, the king promised to punish "without mercy any cursed Jew or heretic."

From 1496 on, Torquemada could barely walk. He rarely left the monastery. He still lived in fear of his enemies. It was said that he kept a unicorn horn and a scorpion tongue nearby when he ate. Both were supposed to be magical cures for poison. On the wall of the monastery, he engraved a phrase in Latin. It read, "Heresies fly like the plague."

Ferdinand and Isabella never forgot Torquemada. They visited him in Ávila in October 1497. During the visit, they received news that their son, Prince Juan, had died. The Spanish rulers had his body brought to Ávila to be buried.

Less than a year later, Torquemada followed Juan to the grave. He was buried in a small chapel in Ávila.

Nearly 300 years later, the Inquisition was still claiming victims. By this time, the courts rarely executed anyone. But in 1826, a man named Cayetano Ripoll was hanged for heresy in Valencia. Eight years later, the queen of Spain finally ended the Inquisition.

For some people, that wasn't enough. In 1836, an angry mob went looking for justice in Ávila. They dug up Torquemada's grave. The bones of the Grand Inquisitor were scattered in the dirt.

TORQUEMADA SPENT HIS FINAL YEARS at
the monastery he built in the walled city of Ávila.
Most of the monastery is still standing today.

BETRAYED

IN 1492, FERDINAND AND ISABELLA promised the Muslims of Granada the freedom to worship as they pleased. That freedom did not last long.

Just seven years later, Spanish priests began converting Muslims. They turned a mosque into a church. Muslim holy texts were burned in a public square.

Muslims in Granada refused to stand by and watch their culture be destroyed. Riots broke out and Spanish soldiers filled the streets of Granada.

The violence gave Ferdinand and Isabella an excuse to break the treaty of 1492. Ferdinand allowed priests to force more Muslims to convert. In October of 1501, a huge bonfire sent thousands more books up in smoke. The following year, Isabella ordered the Muslims of Castile to convert to Christianity—or leave the kingdom. In Aragon, the same order was given in 1525.

Islam had thrived in Spain for 800 years. Now it was all but gone. Thousands of Muslims lived as Christians. They were called *Moriscos*. Like converted Jews, they became targets of the Inquisition.

꒰꒰꒰꒰꒰꒰꒰꒰꒰꒰꒰

Wicked?

꒰꒰꒰꒰꒰꒰꒰꒰꒰꒰꒰

The Spanish Inquisition did its most damaging work during Torquemada's lifetime. The inquisitors had about 2,000 people burned at the stake. They put thousands more in jail. Many more people were humiliated in public. They lost their pride and their friends. Often they lost their property and their jobs. And finally, at Torquemada's insistence, nearly 100,000 Jews were sent into exile. These people lost nearly everything they owned.

Who was the man behind all this suffering? How do we judge what he did? How can we explain a man who had people burned to death in the name of religion?

During Torquemada's time, one fellow Dominican friar called him "the savior of his country." Like many Christians, the friar thought the Inquisition was God's work. In his view, a person's life after death was more important than a person's life on earth. And according to the Bible, people who died as Christians would live forever in heaven. The inquisitors always tried to convince their prisoners to confess their sins. If they succeeded, they did their victims a great service. That, at least, was what Torquemada's supporters thought.

Today, some people point out that the Inquisition was no worse than other courts at the time. All over Europe, common criminals could be tortured. Punishments were terrifying. In France, people could be boiled alive for treason. In England, thieves might be drawn and quartered—killed and cut into pieces—in public.

What, then, sets Torquemada apart? Why does the Spanish Inquisition stand for a certain kind of evil today?

The answer lies in the type of crime Torquemada punished. The people who were punished by the Inquisition hadn't hurt anyone. In fact, we would say they hadn't even committed crimes. They were convicted for their religious beliefs. Under these conditions, no place in Spain was private. Torquemada did not just search homes and read private letters. He reached inside people's minds.

Today, in many countries, laws give people the freedom to worship the way they want. Many people take for granted the right to argue with the leaders of their countries. But even today, there are investigations that go too far. People pry into the private lives of their political enemies. Prosecutors put innocent people in jail when there is a perceived threat to a nation's safety. We have a word for fanatical investigations like these. We call them "inquisitions."

Timeline of Terror

1391

1391: Anti-Jewish riots break out in cities across Spain, including Córdoba, Toledo, Valencia, and Barcelona.

1420: Tomás de Torquemada is born near Valladolid.

1452: Torquemada becomes head of the monastery of Santa Cruz, in the city of Segovia.

1467: Princess Isabella is in Segovia; Torquemada is said to become her teacher.

1469: Isabella of Castile and Ferdinand of Aragon marry.

1474: Isabella becomes queen of Castile.

1477: Queen Isabella moves her court to Seville; starts investigation into conversos.

1478: Pope Sixtus IV issues order granting permission to set up an Inquisition in Spain.

1479: Ferdinand becomes king of Aragon.

1480: Inquisition starts in Spain. Torquemada publishes 37 ways to recognize a heretic.

1482: The pope objects to the inquisitors' tactics in Spain; Ferdinand ignores him.

1483: Torquemada becomes Spain's first Grand Inquisitor and spreads the Inquisition to conversos across Spain.

1484–85: Leaders in Aragon try to resist the Inquisition. Conversos murder inquisitor Pedro de Arbués; this unexpectedly fuels support for the Inquisition.

1492: The Muslim leader of Granada surrenders to Ferdinand and Isabella; later that year, all Jews are ordered to convert or to leave Spain.

1498: Tomás de Torquemada dies.

1498

GLOSSARY

auto-da-fé (AW-toh deh FAY) *noun* ritual of public penance during the Inquisition that included a procession of those found guilty, a church service, an announcement of punishments, and often—burning of those found guilty

Black Death (BLAK DETH) *noun* a disease that killed millions of people in Europe in the 1300s

Catholic (KATH-uh-lik) *noun* a member of the Roman Catholic Church, a Christian church that has the Pope as its leader

convent (KON-vent) *noun* a building where nuns live and work

conversos (kuhn-VURSS-ohs) *noun* Jews who converted to Christianity in medieval Spain

convert (kuhn-VERT) *verb* to change one's religion

ducat (DUHK-et) *noun* a gold coin used throughout Europe during the Middle Ages

effigy (EF-ih-jee) *noun* a crude figure representing a hated person

fanatical (fuh-NAT-ik-uhl) *adjective* wildly enthusiastic about a belief or cause

financier (fi-nanss-IHR) *noun* one who deals with finance and investment

friar (FRY-ur) *noun* a member of a religious order that combines monastic life and outside religious activity.

ghetto (GET-oh) *noun* in 1400s Europe, a separate part of a city where Jews were required to live

gospel (GOSS-puhl) *noun* something accepted as absolute truth

gout (GOWT) *noun* a disease resulting in swollen joints

heresy (HER-uh-see) *noun* a belief or action at odds with the doctrine of the Roman Catholic Church heretic (HER-uh-tik) *noun* a person whose actions or beliefs are considered to be heresy

inquisition (in-kwiz-ISH-in) *noun* an investigation conducted with little regard for individual rights

interrogation (in-ter-uh-GAY-shun) *noun* a formal and detailed questioning session

Jew (JOO) *noun* someone who practices the religion of Judaism

kosher (KOH-shur) *adjective* food that has been prepared according to the laws of the Jewish religion

monastery (MON-uh-ster-ee) *noun* a group of buildings where monks live and work

Moor (MOR) *noun* name used in medieval Spain for a Muslim of North African heritage

Muslim (MUHZ-luhm) *noun* someone who follows the religion of Islam, a religion based on the teachings of Muhammad

penitent (PEN-uh-tuhnt) *noun* a person who repents of sin

prosecutor (PROSS-uh-kyoo-tur) *noun* the person who pursues the formal charges against an accused person during a trial

repent (ri-PENT) *verb* to feel sorry for one's sins

reconciled (REK-uhn-siled) *adjective* forgiven by the Roman Catholic Church

sanbenito (sahn-beh-NEE-toh) *noun* a garment worn by victims of the Spanish Inquisition

speculate (SPEK-yuh-late) *verb* to guess about something without knowing all the facts

synagogue (SIN-a-gog) *noun* a building used by Jewish people for worship

tribunal (trye-BYOO-nuhl) *noun* a panel appointed to make a judgment or inquiry

zealous (ZEL-uhss) *adjective* passionately interested in pursuing something

FIND OUT MORE

Here are some books and Web sites with more information about Tomás de Torquemada and his times.

BOOKS

Melchiore, Susan McCarthy. **The Spanish Inquisition.** Philadelphia: Chelsea House, 2002. (114 pages)
A nicely illustrated overview of the 350 years of the Spanish Inquisition.

Rogers Seavey, Lura. **Spain (Enchantment of the World: Second Series).** New York: Children's Press, 2001. (144 pages)
Information about the history, people, and geography of Spain.

Stewart, Gail B. **Life During the Spanish Inquisition (The Way People Live).** San Diego: Lucent Books, 1998. (96 pages)
An easy-to-read look at the culture of Spain during the Inquisition.

Worth, Richard. **The Spanish Inquisition in World History.** Berkeley Heights, NJ: Enslow Publishers, 2002. (112 pages)
This account of the Inquisition includes excerpts of primary-source documents.

WEB SITES

http://reference.aol.com/columbia/_a/inquisition/20051206055909990021
Columbia Encyclopedia's online article on the Spanish Inquisition

http://www.pbs.org/wnet/heritage/timeline4.html
This timeline of Jewish history, from the PBS series Heritage: Civilization and the Jews, *includes important events from the Inquisition.*

http://www.metmuseum.org/toah/ht/08/eusi/ht08eusi.htm
A political and cultural timeline of the Iberian Peninsula, c.1400-1600, from the Metropolitan Museum of Art

For Grolier subscribers:
http://go.grolier.com/ **searches:** Torquemada; Inquisition; Spain, history of

Index

Authors' Note and Bibliography

Writing about Tomás de Torquemada presents a particular kind of challenge. We know very little about the man himself, until he became involved with the Spanish Inquisition—when he was 58 years old. Yet we want to tell the story of Tomás's entire life, in order to understand what made him do what he did, and to understand his role in the Inquisition.

To do this, we looked at the world in which Tomás grew up. What were the towns like in Spain in the 15th century? What were the religious beliefs back then? How did people get along and interact? By doing this, we can describe what Tomás's life must have been like.

Once Tomás did become the head of the Inquisition in Spain, we have things he wrote that describe the Inquisition. These are mostly in the form of rules. We also have church documents dating from the time of the Inquisition describing what went on. And, finally, we have a few firsthand accounts from witnesses and victims of the Inquisition. From these sources, we pieced together a picture of Tomás.

These books have been most useful in writing and editing Torquemada's story:

Anderson, James M. **Daily Life During the Spanish Inquisition.** Westport, CT: Greenwood Press, 2002.

Hope, Thomas. **Torquemada, Scourge of the Jews: A Biography.** London: G. Allen & Unwin, 1939.

Kagan, Richard L., and Dyer, Abigail, translators and editors. **Inquisitorial Inquiries: Brief Lives of Secret Jews & Other Heretics.** Baltimore: Johns Hopkins Press, 2004.

Kamen, Henry. **The Spanish Inquisition: A Historical Revision.** New Haven: Yale University Press, 1998.

Lowney, Chris. **A Vanished World: Muslims, Christians, and Jews in Medieval Spain.** New York: Free Press, 2005.

Rawlings, Helen. **The Spanish Inquisition.** Malden, MA: Blackwell Publishing, 2006.

Reston, James, Jr. **Dogs of God—Columbus, the Inquisition, and the Defeat of the Moors.** New York: Doubleday, 2005.

Roth, Cecil. **The Spanish Inquisition.** New York: W. W. Norton & Company, 1964.

Sabatini, Rafael. **Torquemada and the Spanish Inquisition: A History.** London: Stanley Paul & Co., undated.

Walsh, William Thomas. **Characters of the Inquisition.** New York: P.J. Kenedy and Sons, 1940.

Special thanks to our editor, Tod Olson.

—Enid A. Goldberg and Norman Itzkowitz